MW01146606

# The Tuskegee Airmen: The History and Legacy of America's First Black Fighter Pilots in World War II

## By Charles River Editors

**Toni Frissell's picture of Tuskegee airman Edward M. Thomas**

## About Charles River Editors

**Charles River Editors** provides superior editing and original writing services across the digital publishing industry, with the expertise to create digital content for publishers across a vast range of subject matter. In addition to providing original digital content for third party publishers, we also republish civilization's greatest literary works, bringing them to new generations of readers via ebooks.

Sign up here to receive updates about free books as we publish them, and visit Our Kindle Author Page to browse today's free promotions and our most recently published Kindle titles.

# Introduction

**An advertisement poster depicting a Tuskegee airman**

## The Tuskegee Airmen

"When World War II started, the black press and the black community wanted blacks to be able to fly because in 1925, the military had done a study that said that blacks didn't have the intelligence, ability, or coordination to fly airplanes. The pressure from the NAACP and the press caused them to start an experimental group that was to be trained in Tuskegee, Alabama, and that's why we were known as 'The Tuskegee Airmen.'…I come from a generation of African Americans where we were always trying to be better. We were taught that you had to be better than whites in order to move ahead, so we were very competitive…Practically everyone in the Tuskegee Airmen was an exceptional scholar and athlete, so the competition was really great and it helped to bond us together." – Roscoe Brown, a pilot for the Tuskegee Airmen

The United States has no shortage of famous military units, from the Civil War's Iron Brigade to the 101st Airborne, but one would be hard pressed to find one that had to go through as many hardships off the field as the Tuskegee Airmen, a group of African American fighter pilots who overcame Jim Crow at home and official segregation in the military to serve their country in the final years of World War II. In fact, it required a concerted effort by groups such as the National Association for the Advancement of Colored People (NAACP) and the extreme circumstances brought about by World War II that the military eventually decided to establish the "Tuskegee Experiment."

The black crews trained at Tuskegee before being sent overseas, and even then, they faced discrimination from those who didn't trust them to do more than escort bombers flown by white pilots. However, as the men proved their worth in the heat of battle, some of the squadrons' red markings helped them earn the nickname "Red Tails," and their track record was so good that eventually the white pilots of American bombers wanted to fly with them. As Tuskegee airman Roscoe Brown eloquently put it, "They have a saying that excellence is the antidote to prejudice; so, once you show you can do it, some of the barriers will come down."

In time, the Tuskegee Airmen would be romanticized and mythologized to the extent that it was erroneously claimed that some escort squadrons didn't lose a bomber to the enemy, which led Tuskegee airman Grant Williams to note in jest, "Back then, nobody realized the significance of what we were doing. Now, they seem to think we could walk on water." However, even though the suggestion that the escorts lost no bombers on their missions was inaccurate, there is no question the Tuskegee Airmen's record was elite and some of the fighter pilots were among the best to serve. Ironically, this was a byproduct of the systemic racism the men had to overcome, which resulted in extra training and planning among other issues.

*The Tuskegee Airmen: The History and Legacy of America's First Black Fighter Pilots in World War II* chronicles the story of the Tuskegee Airmen and their important place in American military history. Along with pictures of important people, places, and events, you will learn about the Tuskegee Airmen like never before, in no time at all.

The Tuskegee Airmen: The History and Legacy of America's First Black Fighter Pilots in World War II

About Charles River Editors

Introduction

## Chapter 1: Air Corps Policy Remained As Before

"Blacks served in the American military virtually from the founding of the nation, although pre-Civil War policies placed severe limitations on their participation. During the Civil War, the Army began raising black regiments, but with white officers, and a policy of racial segregation prevailed for almost a century thereafter. During World War I, the Air Service, the Air Corps' predecessor, excluded blacks entirely in the belief that they were unfit for aviation duty, an exclusion that remained the official Air Corps policy for over twenty years after the war ended. The federal government's policy began to change in 1939 when Congress ordered the Air Corps to accept blacks into the Civilian Pilot Training Program (CPTP), a program designed to provide a cadre of trained pilots should the country suddenly be plunged into war. The first year, almost one hundred black pilots completed the course of training, but the Air Corps refused to accept any of them. Air Corps policy remained as before: whites and blacks could not be integrated and there were no plans to create segregated units. Nevertheless, the CPTP was an important first step. During the course of World War II, over two thousand blacks completed CPTP, and most of those who eventually became AAF pilots got at least a part of their training in that way." – An excerpt from "Air Force Officers Personnel Policy Development, 1944-1977."

The roots of the Tuskegee Airmen run deep, all the way back to the first combat planes flown during World War I, but like many roots involving black soldiers in American history, they were heavily obscured. When the United States began training pilots for World War I, a number of African American men, knowing full well they'd never be allowed to train as pilots, applied to be aerial observers, only to be rejected by the white officers sitting behind government desks.

As Ulysses Lee noted in *The Employment of Negro* Troops, during the two decades that separated the Great War and World War II, black men continued to fight for the right to fly only to receive replies such as the following: "In time of peace the Army must be so organized as to assure a balanced force, containing, in the proper proportions, elements of all arms and services, and capable of rapid and orderly expansion in time of war without major changes in the basic peacetime organization. Consequently, it is necessary to set up specific units to which colored personnel may be assigned, and these organizations must have a definite and proper place in the balanced force organizations of the Army as a whole. These organizations now include units of the infantry, cavalry, quartermaster corps, and medical corps. They meet our peacetime requirements, and provide the necessary nucleus for wartime expansion." At other times, the reply was more forceful: "Your remarks and the contents of the accompanying paper have been carefully noted. However, under a long established rule the War Department refrains from participation in controversial discussions arising from time to time in connection with articles appearing in the press, or statements made by public speakers or debaters, when the activities of the Army or its personnel are subjected to criticism."

While such responses may have tried to sugarcoat rejections by arguing that their policies were about unit cohesion, Lee also pointed out that the War Department was unabashed in its racist beliefs. For example, it also claimed the Army Air Corps "gathered in men of technical and mechanical experience and ability. As a rule, the colored man has not been attracted to this field in the same way or to the same extent as the white man. Particularly is this so of aerial engineering…many white applicants are being denied places." In response to these kinds of blanket rejections, the secretary of the NAACP was eventually compelled to complain, "It is obvious that colored men cannot be attracted to the field of aviation 'in the same way or to the same extent as the white man' when the door to that field is slammed in the colored man's face . . . . There are thousands of excellent colored mechanics in the country and if the War Department did not prejudice the case by definitely excluding them, we feel sure that there would be no difficulty in finding and developing men with all the qualifications required of pilots, mechanics, and all the other functions included in the air service."

Senator Henry H. Schwartz, long a proponent of recruiting African Americans into the Air Corps, introduced an amendment to a bill aimed specifically at allowing black men to train to be pilots, and he defended it on March 7, 1939 by saying, "Somebody may say, 'There is no provision in the bill now which would prevent a Negro receiving such training,' but…I can only judge the future by the past. I believe the situation is such that unless we give this specific and affirmative recognition, possibly our qualified Negro citizens will not have an opportunity to become air pilots." That amendment passed on April 3, 1939 and read, "The Secretary of War is authorized, in his discretion and under the rules, regulations, and limitations to be prescribed by him, to lend to accredited civilian aviation schools, one or more of which shall be designated by the Civil Aeronautics Authority for the training of any Negro air pilot, at which personnel of the Military Establishment are pursuing a course of education and training pursuant to detail thereto under competent orders of the War Department, out of aircraft, aircraft parts, aeronautical equipment and accessories for the Air Corps, on hand and belonging to the Government, such articles as may appear to be required for instruction, training, and maintenance purposes."

**Schwartz**

Many of the black pilots would come into the armed services via the Civilian Pilot Training Programs (CPTP) founded around the country during the last years of the 1930s. There were CPTP programs at several traditionally black universities, including Hampton University, Virginia State, Delaware State, and Howard. The most famous, of course, was the program located at Tuskegee University in Alabama. One school leader later said, "[I knew they] would do their best and put everything they had in the instruction. But I was frankly interested in [Tuskegee's aviation students] making the best record possible on the examination and felt teachers with considerable training and experience in aeronautics would make the difference in the results of the examination."

At first, it seemed that the Army might try to resist allowing African American pilots to serve, but Schwartz remained determined. At one point, when two generals were complaining about not being able to recruit good men, Schwartz said to them, "Of course, you understand the same as I do, whether we want to admit it or not, that back under this is a feeling in the Army and in the Navy that bringing these Negro pilots and giving them this opportunity will result in some embarrassment one way or another on account of social or economic conditions. ... I hope the committee will amend the bill because I do think the War Department needs a little urging."

As part of the planning to prepare in the event America joined World War II, the Army Air Corps created a psychological research unit at Maxwell Air Field in Montgomery, Alabama, and the unit's mission was to test and train pilots and other fliers for service in case of war. It was determined that the same testing and training should be given to all the cadets, regardless of their race, and the standards were understandably high given that training and outfitting a flier was an expensive proposition.

Black candidates flocked to the area hoping for a chance to show that they could excel, one of whom was Charles Alfred Anderson of Pennsylvania. Knowing he would never receive proper training in the early 20th century, Anderson eventually bought his own plane and had to teach himself to take off and land. Under these conditions, he had been training and flying for years, often under very adverse circumstances, before arriving in Alabama. Ernest Buehl, the German born instructor who eventually started helping Anderson fly, recalled, "In them days a colored man in an airplane, it just never was known. Anderson had been to all the other airports surrounding Philadelphia. People really condemned him and called him names. But, oh boy, how he would like to fly. When the government agent came [to license him] he took me aside and he called me everything under the sun because I would even attempt to get that man into an airplane. I finally tell him, 'Look, I'm a foreigner. I'm a citizen by the paper. That guy's born here.' And I threatened to make a little trouble for this guy. So he finally took him up and kept him up a considerable time longer than a white man. He really put him through the works."

**Anderson**

After some years of working as a flight instructor in Virginia, Anderson was recruited in 1940 to head up the training program at Tuskegee, and it was there, in March 1941, that he made a historic flight. First Lady Eleanor Roosevelt was visiting Tuskegee when she asked to review the school's aviation program, so she was taken out to the facility and introduced to Anderson, who remembered, "First thing she said was, 'I always heard colored people couldn't fly airplanes.' She was amazed." Defying protocol, Anderson asked if she'd like to go up for a ride, and she surprised everyone by accepting his offer. He explained, "While we were up there, she told me she had planned to take flying lessons herself with Amelia Earhart." When they returned to the ground, Eleanor reportedly said, "Well, you can fly all right." The story of her flight with the black pilot made the papers, along with a picture of them together, and the Tuskegee program got a huge boost of publicity and goodwill. Once she was back in Washington, she used her influence to raise a $175,000 loan, which was then used to build Moton Field, a place where the men could take their initial training.

**Eleanor Roosevelt and Anderson**

**A picture of training pilots at Moton during the war**

Over time, the opportunity to fly attracted black men from other military units, and in March 1941, the War Department created the 99th Pursuit Squadron, the first flying unit made up of black pilots. The unit was initially stationed out of Chanute Field in Rantoul, Illinois and started with a class of 271 men, who were to be trained in the skills needed to fly and keep planes flying during wartime. Meanwhile, the Tuskegee program was also up and running by June 1941, and 47 officers and 429 enlisted men were training there by the time the United States entered World War II.

**A picture of Tuskegee airmen in 1942 or 1943**

**The 99th Squadron's patch**

## Chapter 2: Far-Reaching Changes

"More far-reaching changes came during the presidential election of 1940, when President Franklin D. Roosevelt found his campaign hampered by an economic depression that had not yet completely run its course, controversy over his attempt for a third term, and an isolationist backlash against policies that favored the British in the war that had started the previous September. For the first time in a presidential election, he faced a serious challenge from the Republican candidate (in 1940, Wendell Willkie). To strengthen his standing among minority voters, the president made a number of campaign promises, including one to establish black flying units in the Air Corps. Following his election victory, Roosevelt ordered the formation of the all-black 99th Fighter Squadron (Separate) with ground personnel only. To furnish the rated personnel for the new unit, pilot training began at Tuskegee Institute, a black college near Montgomery, Alabama." – An excerpt from "Air Force Officers Personnel Policy Development, 1944-1977"

All Americans are familiar with the "day that will live in infamy." At 9:30 a.m. on Sunday, December 7, 1941, Pearl Harbor, the advanced base of the United States Navy's Pacific Fleet, was ablaze. It had been smashed by aircraft launched by the carriers of the Imperial Japanese Navy. All eight battleships had been sunk or badly damaged, 350 aircraft had been knocked out, and over 2,000 Americans lay dead. Indelible images of the USS *Arizona* exploding and the USS *Oklahoma* capsizing and floating upside down have been ingrained in the American conscience ever since. In less than an hour and a half the Japanese had almost wiped out America's entire naval presence in the Pacific.

On December 8, 1941, a day after Pearl Harbor, President Franklin D. Roosevelt addressed Congress and the nation the following day, giving a stirring speech seeking a declaration of war against Japan. The beginning lines of the speech are instantly familiar, with Roosevelt forever marking Pearl Harbor in the national conscience as "a date which will live in infamy." Congress voted overwhelmingly in support of an immediate declaration of war: 82-0 in the Senate and 388-1 in the House. Churchill had said that Britain would declare war "within the hour" if Japan attacked America. There was no way that the British were going to forget the support they had already received from Roosevelt. Britain was at war with Japan the same day. The other Axis powers quickly followed suit, with Germany and Italy declaring war on America and vice versa by December 11.

## President Roosevelt signs the declaration of war against Japan

Meanwhile, the isolationist America First Committee instantly became a thing of the past, and the United States began fully mobilizing almost overnight, thanks to the peacetime draft Roosevelt had implemented. The bill helped the country's armed forces swell by two million within months of Pearl Harbor. In 1942 alone, six million men headed off to North Africa, Great Britain and the Pacific Ocean, carrying weapons in one hand and pictures of pin-up models like Betty Grable in the other.

Once war broke out, it was imperative that Tuskegee Army Airfield get up and running as soon as possible. A $5.7 million contract was awarded to McKissack and McKissack, Inc., to build the field, and more than 2,000 men worked nearly round the clock to complete the field in only six months. They also completed the state of the art hangars, designed by Tuskegee student Booker Conley.

After the field's completion, Captain Benjamin Davis, one of only two black officers in the Army, took over training the pilots, acting under Colonel Frederick von Kimble. Kimble believed in keeping the peace in order to allow his men to focus on their training rather than conflicts with those living around them, so he abided by local laws concerning segregation and insisted his men did as well. This brought him under fire from his superiors until he was replaced by Major Noel F. Parrish, previously the Tuskegee Airfield's director of instruction. Parrish proved to be the perfect man for the job and was instrumental in convincing Congress to let the pilots serve in combat zones. He also remained a supporter of Civil Rights after the war, writing in 1946, "In the administration of segregated units there is no routine. There can be no consistent segregation of policy not because it was immoral but because it was wasteful and impossible to implement logically and consistently." Benjamin Davis later heaped praise on Parrish, noting that he "may have been the only white person who believed that blacks could learn to fly airplanes. ... When Parrish first arrived at Tuskegee, the so-called Army Air Corps experiment (in black aviation) was in its beginning stages, and Parrish had a single, vitally important, crucial job to do...He had to prove that black people could fly airplanes, and not only fly them but have the same standard that the Army Air Corps demanded of its white pilot applicants. ... [He] had to move across the line between his white subordinates and the black students, and he was carefully watched by the national black press. The job probably gave him fits, but he did a brilliant job."

**Parrish**

**Davis at Tuskegee in 1942**

Charles McGee remembered the day he learned the United States had been attacked by the Japanese: "My father was preaching in a church in Gary, Indiana, in 1941, and I had taken a summer job in the steel mill there. I was also in the Coleridge Taylor Glee Club. We were driving to sing at a church in south Chicago at 4 that Sunday afternoon when we heard the news of the attack on Pearl Harbor. We went on with the show, but I knew that one way or another we were going to be involved in the war."

**A portrait of McGee as a Tuskegee airman**

More importantly, for McGee and many others, beginning of the war with Japan opened a door to new dreams for the future. As Roscoe Brown noted, "When World War II started, the black press and the black community wanted blacks to be able to fly because in 1925, the military had done a study that said that blacks didn't have the intelligence, ability, or coordination to fly airplanes. The pressure from the NAACP and the press caused them to start an experimental group that was to be trained in Tuskegee, Alabama, and that's why we were known as 'The Tuskegee Airmen.' They went to colleges and recruited the best leaders and athletes to be Tuskegee Airmen. When I was attending Springfield College in Springfield, Mass., my junior year, where I was valedictorian of my class, I had already earned a commission as an infantry officer when I was 18 because they had R.O.T.C. when I was in high school. I resigned my commission, signed up to be a Tuskegee Airman..."

McGee had a similar recollection: "I don't recall even seeing an airplane when I was young. It was about the time I was in college that the Army was beginning to recruit nonflying personnel– communications, engineering, armament and mechanics–for a one-squadron black experiment at Chanute Field. Word of that was spreading through the black community. Well, I already had a draft card, so I filled in that pilot's application. I was sent over to a couple of places in Indiana to take the examination, and when I passed that, in April 1942, I had to take a physical. I'd also been going with a girl from Champaign, Illinois, Frances E. Nelson, and that summer we became engaged. In my expectation of the call to arms, I did not go back to school in September–I continued working. Frances and I were married on Saturday, October 17, and Monday morning's mail had that letter I knew was going to come. On October 27, I was sworn into the enlisted reserve, and a few weeks later, I got the call to go to Tuskegee."

Still, Parrish was only one man and prejudice ran deep in the United States. As indicated by the "Air Force Officers Personnel Policy Development, 1944-1977), the Tuskegee Airmen and other minorities faced steep issues at the beginning of the war: "After the United States entered World War II, the AAF agreed to take a percentage of blacks, but could find few ways to employ them productively. Almost 85 percent scored in the lowest two (of five) categories on the classification examinations, the result of poor educations, economic deprivation, and cultural poverty. Many served in racially segregated Aviation Squadrons, performing manual labor under the supervision of white officers. Others ended up in segregated supply, medical, or transportation units, also supervised by white officers. A limited number received training through normal schools as navigators, bombardiers, and nonrated officers where, unlike the Tuskegee program, the actual training was integrated, although living and dining accommodations for the races were separate. At no time did the number of black officers exceed 1,500 (of a total of over 380,000), and, as a matter of policy, none commanded white subordinates. The only organizations with black officers in positions of responsibility were the segregated flying units."

Not surprisingly, Tuskegee itself shocked those who were arriving in the Deep South for the first time. McGee explained, "The trip down was my first real experience of the South. As the train left southern Illinois, you had to change your location in the car. We knew there were certain barber shops or restaurants to go to in Chicago, but you could feel the change in atmosphere and approach as you entered the Deep South–you knew that whatever happened, the law was not going to uphold whatever your position was. When you were a black man from the North, you especially had to be careful what you said and did. You learned to be extra careful when stopping to fill up your car, and even avoid some filling stations. To a degree, the southern blacks were concerned about how a northern Negro was going to act, and a lot of conversations dealt with what you needed to know and where to go to keep out of trouble. One of my classmates happened to be from a well-to-do family who owned a drug store in Montgomery, Alabama, and he helped steer me into the black community, because you didn't go into the downtown area very much."

Roscoe Brown described just how organized the segregation was in Tuskegee, and how much it aggravated the minorities training there: "Everything was black or white. They wouldn't let black officers in the white officers' club. Someone tried to enforce segregation on the base when we moved to Walterboro, South Carolina, for our combat training. We went to the movie theater and they had a sign up that said 'blacks in the back.' We wouldn't tolerate that, so we went and sat up in the front of the white section. An MP came by and said, 'We'll court-martial you if you don't move.' We said, 'The government has spent $75,000 training us, so I don't think they'd appreciate us being court-martialed for standing up for our citizen's rights.' The next day, the signs were down."

Some would later question the Army's decision to locate the training center in Alabama, but McGee understood the reasons. "In those days, there was a great fear around the country that when you get large groups of blacks together, there's got to be trouble. There were places in the North, like Colorado, California and Illinois, that were turned down for the location. On the other hand, the Tuskegee Institute had already had a successful civilian pilot training program, so when the Army began its 99th Squadron experiment, Tuskegee, with flight instructors who began flying in the 1930s, got the contract. By the time I got to Tuskegee in the fall of 1942, the airfield had been completed, although they had been training on it even while it was under construction. The 99th had completed its 33-pilot cadre by the time I got there."

Those training the Tuskegee pilots ran into another problem caused by segregation because when other black Army units decided to dump unwanted personnel, they tended to send them to Tuskegee. This meant that there were often not enough jobs to keep men busy, leading to idleness and boredom. Those completing training often did not receive their officer's commissions in a timely manner, since, according to the Commanding General of the U.S. Army Air Forces, Henry "Hap" Arnold, "Negro pilots cannot be used in our present Air Corps units since this would result in Negro officers serving over white enlisted men creating an impossible social situation."

**Arnold**

Ironically, one of the things that broke down walls for other African Americans within the ranks was the nature of the training the men were receiving. For instance, pilots needed flight surgeons, and thus African American physicians had to be brought in to care for them since the races had to remain segregated. These doctors were made officers because of their educations, adding to the number of black officers in the United States Army. While the first doctors had to receive their training through a correspondence course, the U.S. Army School of Aviation Medicine allowed two black doctors in during 1943. Throughout the 1940s, 17 flight surgeons served the Tuskegee Airmen, each averaging a four year tour of duty.

## Chapter 3: Trainees

"Chief among the first trainees was Capt. (later Lt. Gen.) Benjamin O. Davis, Jr., the first of his race to graduate from West Point in this century and the son of the first black general in American military history. Although the Tuskegee school was beset with chronic racial tensions, ranging from outright hostility from the local civilian population to black resentment at the all-white staff, over nine hundred pilots graduated by the end of the war." – An excerpt from "Air Force Officers Personnel Policy Development, 1944-1977."

Most of the men had dreamed of flying for their entire lives, and many had thought that it was a dream that might never come true, so there was a sense of awe and joy about finally getting in the air. However, there were also a number of surprises, as Roscoe Brown remembered: "Because magazines would talk about flying, we thought we actually knew how to fly! You go down, you go up. We got our first ride in a small plane with an instructor pilot, and then in a biplane and it was open cockpit so you got the feeling it was really like flying. Once you got into the military planes, it was a question of learning your precision—how you could make turns, land the planes. Some of us were better than others. Of the 3,000 who trained to be pilots at Tuskegee, about 1,000 of us graduated. About 650 were single-engine pilots, and the balance was bomber pilots who never got to be in combat. Of the 650 single-engine pilots, about 400 of us went overseas and flew missions…"

Like many men, McGee had to become acclimated to life in the air, particularly the way the plane moved and swayed. He admitted, "I remember having a queasy stomach in the first few flights and talking to the flight surgeon, who just said, 'Quit eating fried foods for breakfast.' I did, and I never had another problem. My first check was on February 11, 1943, and the lieutenant said it was unsatisfactory. I had two more flights with an instructor, then tried again on February 14 and passed the check. We used Eglin Army Air Field in Florida for gunnery training. I finished my last flying in the AT-6 on June 25, graduated on June 30, and on July 6 I had my first Curtiss P-40 ride. I also took blind flying in the AT-6, to improve my instrument proficiency. I qualified as expert in gunnery but not nearly as well with handguns."

**The North American T-6 Texan during World War II**

**A Curtiss P-40**

After completing the first stage of their training at Moton, the men were next taken to Tuskegee Army Air Field, located about 10 miles from the school, and within months of America going to war, there were more than 3,000 African American soldiers stationed there. McGee described the scene: "At that time, too, Colonel Noel F. Parrish was the white commander. The previous commander, Colonel Frederick Von Kimble, was not very supportive of the program, but he was relieved and replaced by Parrish, who had been directing operations. He believed in the program and the people. I entered preflight training as part of Class 43-G, but I was one of several who skipped upper preflight, perhaps because of my college studies, and ended up graduating in Class 43-F. Primary training was at Moton Field, a grass strip just outside the city of Tuskegee, in the Stearman PT-17. We then went on the Army airfield, which was where our white instructors were. We did basic training in the Vultee BT-13A and advanced training in the North American AT-6. My wife came down and worked as a secretary for a Dr. Kenny in the Tuskegee Institute hospital while I was going through training, but I usually only saw her on Sunday afternoons."

In addition to the better known fighter pilots, bomber crews also received training at Tuskegee. At first, the training was sporadic, but over time, the training settled into a regular pattern.

McGee explained, "I think the first twin-engine instruction had already begun in the summer of 1943. Twin-engine pilot training started in the Beech AT-10 Wichita–what a clunker–then we switched to the North American TB-25J, a stripped-down B-25J. That was a marvelous plane, with great big radial engines, a lot more power–a wonderful training platform."

Once the pilots were being trained, the NAACP was able to exert enough pressure on the federal government to have them formally organized into a bombing unit. On May 13, 1943, the Air Corps officially formed the 616th Bombardment Squadron, making it the "feeder" squadron for the 477th Bombardment Group. Unfortunately, the 477th was only active for six weeks before it was made inactive; by this time, more and more of the cadets were dropping out of the program, unable to withstand the pressure of the hostile environment. By the end of September, there were more than 200 unemployed cadets on the base, placing a heavy burden on its resources.

Thankfully, the government reactivated the 477th in January 1944, and in time, it came to consist of a total of four bomber squadrons made up of 1,200 men flying 60 B-25 Mitchell bombers. Later, the 477th would include the 617th, 618th and 619th squadrons. The men's primary training field was Selfridge Field near Detroit, but the twin-engine pilots began their training at Tuskegee while the ground crews trained at Mather Field in California. Meanwhile, the gunners trained at nearby Eglin Field, just south of the state line in Northwest Florida.

As this suggests, black crews were training at a number of other fields across the country, but thanks to the fighter pilots' exploits in combat, Tuskegee would always be considered the home of the black flying units.

### Chapter 4: Combat-Ready Status

"With the United States in the war, officials were in a quandary over how to use the 99th Fighter Squadron once it achieved combat-ready status. Many senior military and government officials viewed flight training for blacks as a politically motivated experiment, an experiment that was likely to fail. These same officials questioned whether blacks had the capability to lead and were skeptical that blacks could perform a combat role. Accordingly, the AAF considered converting the 99th to multiengine aircraft for marine patrol missions from bases on the west coast of Africa, an assignment consistent with the Army policy of assigning the few black officers in its ranks to predominately black nations as military attaches. These plans were scuttled, however, when the invasion of North Africa in November 1942 created a sudden demand for more fighter squadrons. The 99th, commanded by Lt. Col. Benjamin O. Davis, Jr., arrived in Morocco in April 1943. Initially, the unit, inexperienced (no pilot had been rated for more than a year), undermanned, and flying obsolescent aircraft (P-40s), was no match for the battle-hardened Luftwaffe units it faced. Individual pilots fought with skill and courage, but they simply did not have the experience necessary to master the more difficult task of flying and fighting as members of a formation. Losses were high, and the unit failed to destroy a single enemy aircraft in the last half of 1943." – An excerpt from "Air Force Officers Personnel Policy Development, 1944-1977."

Since America was in the midst of war not only in Pacific but also across the Atlantic in North Africa in 1942, the new pilots' training was expedited, and those who passed were soon moved on to other fields. For the Tuskegee Airmen who were part of one of the fighter squadrons, these postings were merely temporary spots on the way to the war zones overseas. McGee explained, "I left Tuskegee in August for squadron and group formation flying and aerobatics at Selfridge Field, Michigan, where the 100th, 301st and 302nd squadrons of the 332nd Fighter Group were being formed. We were fully combat ready in the P-40L and P-40N by October–and that's when the decision was made that the group was going to fly the Bell P-39Q. It had the engine in the back and had less horsepower than the P-40, but we young pilots just used to say, 'If the crew chief can start it, then I can fly it.' We trained on P-39s through November, and in early December we left Selfridge Field by train under classified orders, arriving at Newport News, Virginia. We left Newport News on a big convoy that zigzagged across the Atlantic and into the Mediterranean. My ship, with the 302nd Squadron, went to Taranto, Italy, then we trucked over to the Naples area, where we began flying from Montecorvino."

On April 2, 1943, the 99th Fighter Squadron left Tuskegee and headed for North Africa. There they reported to Colonel William Momyer, in command of the 33rd Fighter Group. They finally saw action that May as Allied planes attacked the island of Pantelleria in preparation for the coming amphibious invasion of Sicily. As a result of their efforts, more than 11,000 Italians surrendered the garrison, the first time in history that an island had surrendered as a result of air attack only. In recognition of their efforts, the men were awarded a Distinguished Unit Citation.

**Momyer**

A picture of crewmen in the 99th arming a plane

**A picture of mechanics in the 99th**

In February 1944, another group of pilots, the 332nd Fighter Group, left Tuskegee. It consisted of three squadrons: the 100th, the 301st and the 302nd. According to McGee, "Usually, each squadron would have 18 aircraft takeoff–16 and two spares. If everything went well as we climbed and formed up, the group leader would tell the spares to go on back to base. But if anyone was having engine trouble, then the spares would go wherever needed. The commander of the 302nd was Captain Edward C. Gleed. After he became group operations officer, the squadron was led by 1st Lt. Melvin T. 'Red' Jackson, then V.V. Haywood. In September 1944, I was promoted to first lieutenant and became a flight leader. Sometimes the squadron commander or operations officer led the formations, sometimes the group operations officer, and when the leader had a problem, someone next in line would be designated to assume the lead."

The men of the 332nd Fighter Group traveled to Italy, where they joined the 99th at Ramitelli Airfield on the Adriatic Sea. There they spent most of their time patrolling the already secured coast of Italy. Somewhat understandably, McGee noted that this proved to be less than exciting for those wanting a taste of action: "We began operations on February 14, 1944, patrolling Naples Harbor to the Isle of Capri, and we also did coastal patrol. My first patrol was on February 28. We moved up to Capodichino on March 4, and did the rest of our tactical patrolling from there. The P-39Q was too slow and essentially a low-altitude aircraft–we flew at 10,000 to

15,000 feet, and by the time we reached even that altitude to intercept intruders, they were usually back in Germany. It was frustrating. Meanwhile, the men of the 99th were flying their P-40s with the 79th Fighter Group and shot down several aircraft over Anzio, earning the right to be called fighter pilots."

**Pictures of the 332nd Fighting Group in Ramitelli, Italy**

Nevertheless, their missions during the Battle of Monte Cassino earned the men a second Distinguished Unit Citation, and McGee subsequently described the group's contributions in May 1944: "[May 5] was the day I first flew the Republic P-47D Thunderbolt. An even bigger day was May 23, when the group moved to Ramitelli on the Adriatic side and we began long-range escort flights. They took a farmer's field, set up headquarters in the farmhouse, laid down pierced-steel planking, set up a couple of squadrons on one side of the field with their tents, and one on the other. P-47D No. 280 was assigned me for most of my flights at that time. It was just after that time that the 99th was assigned to the 332nd Fighter Group, so all four of the black squadrons were together."

**Picture of an Allied bomber over Monte Cassino**

It probably seemed to make sense to war planners to have black fighter pilots from different squadrons stationed near each other, but there were problems with this new arrangement, as McGee noted: "Well, you see, [the 99th] had been in combat about a year, and we had only been there five months. They also felt that they had achieved a certain degree of integration by flying with the 33rd and 79th groups. Even though the 33rd's commander, Colonel William Momyer, didn't like them and his reports were all mediocre, the 79th's Colonel Earl E. Bates saw them as more pilots for his group and let them operate alongside the rest of his squadrons. The 332nd Group's commander, Colonel Benjamin O. Davis, Jr., had commanded the 99th, and they were pleased to be serving under him again, but there was a little resentment among their more experienced pilots over the fact that the other squadron commanders and group staff had already been picked. But B.O. [Davis] was very strong, sincere and severe–he laid down the law and things moved along."

**Benjamin Davis in Sicily as part of the 332<sup>nd</sup> Group**

**Members of the 332nd being briefed in Sicily**

**Picture of a crewman in the 332nd rearming a plane in Sicily**

Finally, the men of the 332nd got their wish when they were assigned escort duty for the 15th Air Force and charged with seeing to it that the bombers made their way safely from Ramitelli to their targets in southern Germany and southeast Europe. McGee explained, "In May they decided we were going to go to the Fifteenth Air Force. As the Allies advanced north, the bombers came up from Africa to bases in Italy, but they were getting their tails shot off over targets like Ploesti [oil fields in Romania], so four single-engine fighter groups were picked for the escort. There were the candy-striped 31st, the yellow-tailed 52nd, the 'checker-tail clan' of the 325th and the red-tailed 332nd."

**Pictures of one of the escort pilots handing a ring to a crewman before escorting for the 15th Air Force**

Over time, the men also received better aircraft. When asked about his first combat mission, McGee mentioned the various planes then in service: "That was a mission to Munich on June 13, and my feeling was, 'We're finally doing the job we came to do.' We were still flying the P-47, and for such long-range penetration missions, we'd usually have a group carry the bombers out and another group would take them back. The P-47 was fine with B-24s, but not so good with the B-17, which could fly higher in an attempt to avoid anti-aircraft fire. We always liked to be a couple thousand feet above the bomber stream to do our S-turning, but even when its supercharger cut in at 19,000 feet, the P-47 would become sluggish trying to get above the highest B-17s. All that changed on July 1, when I took my first flight in the North American P-51C-10. I flew my first long-range mission in the Mustang on July 4, escorting bombers to Romania. We could take a P-51 up to 35,000 feet and it would still be maneuverable. My usual P-51C was 42-103072, which as I recall bore the 'buzz number' 78. I christened it Kitten, which was my wife's nickname, and my crew chief, Nathaniel Wilson, kept it purring, too."

**A picture of P-51 Mustangs during the war**

According to his daughter, the P-51 Mustang also particularly pleased airman Joseph Gomer, "The 301st then traded in their P-39 Cobras for the P-47 Thunderbolt, a seven ton fighter that impressed them with its sheer size. While it was a good dependable fighter, according to my father, it didn't compare to the sleek P-51 Mustang which the unit later received. It was his dream aircraft and his favorite. His unit kept busy, and while in Italy it flew 1,500 sorties and downed 111 enemy aircraft including the sinking of one German navy destroyer while losing 78 pilots of their own through accidents, training, and combat. Four of the casualties were his tent mates, so a ground officer was put in his tent to keep him company. He himself had a few close calls. He crash-landed a P-39, lost his P-51 canopy, and was bullet ridden in a P-47 by a Me-109 German Fighter. He looked out of his cockpit in time to see a line of 20mm cannon holes stitch his wing right to the fuselage. As the German aircraft flew past him, he remembers seeing the swastika on its tail assembly 'big as day.'"

The combat missions typically consisted of what more than one pilot described as hours of boredom punctuated with minutes of sheer terror. McGee insisted, "They were all long flights, usually five hours and at least one I recall that was six hours. On those flights, you find that the cockpit really gets small and you can sweat through a leather flight jacket sitting up there under the sun. We were glad when we got off the target and we could be less rigid in keeping formation with one another. Fighter sweeps were great fun. I first saw Messerschmitt Me-109s over Markersdorf, Austria, on July 26, 1944. In his briefings, B.O. was very explicit about the way we operated. If enemy planes appeared to attack, the flight commander would designate who would go after them. The rest of us stayed with the bombers, doing S-maneuvers, and we were glad that we weren't bomber pilots, who had to hold a tight formation as they made their final runs over the target, through enemy flak and fighters. On this occasion, the Germans didn't attack the formation. In another sighting, 2nd Lt. Roger Romine was told to get them and got a kill."

### Chapter 5: More Time to Prove Itself

"In September 1943, Col. (later, Gen.) William W. Momyer, commander of the 33d Fighter Group of which the 99th was a part, asked that the 99th be withdrawn from combat. He did not believe that the unit had the aggressiveness or desire for combat necessary in a first-rate flying organization. Senior AAF officers, seeing the request as verification of their doubts that blacks could perform in combat, supported Momyer's request. General Arnold also agreed with the recommendation, but, worried about the political implications, asked General Marshall to discuss the matter with the President before reaching a final decision. Instead, Marshall ordered that the 99th be given more time to prove itself." – An excerpt from "Air Force Officers Personnel Policy Development, 1944-1977."

Combat gave the Tuskegee Airmen an opportunity to do more than defeat their enemy; it also gave them a chance to score a hit against prejudice in the United States and elsewhere. Brown noted, "The most difficult part…[was] overcoming the negative beliefs about blacks that we couldn't do certain things. Our training was relatively fair; however, once we went into combat, initially they didn't want us to be in the high-responsibility positions escorting the bombers. Once they realized they were losing so many bombers, they wanted as many people as possible to escort them; we were given that mission, and we did it extremely well. Then, once people began to hear about us, they said, 'We want those guys, they're really good!' We were probably as good as many of the white pilots, but many of the white pilots would leave the bombers and shoot down planes to become heroes; our commander insisted that we stay with the bombers, which is why the bombers would like seeing our Red Tails flying over them."

Indeed, the men accumulated an impressive record and the "Red Tails" soon became a welcome sight among those making their way to Germany. When asked how the unit came to choose red for their marking, McGee relayed the following tale: "As I understand it, red paint was what was readily available. I think on the first couple of planes they just painted the rudder, but one of the pilots in the 332nd said, 'That's not enough.' As it turned out, the gunners on the Boeing B-17s and Consolidated B-24s loved it because they could easily tell who was friendly at high altitude over the target area."

**Max Haynes' photos of a P-51 Mustang with the distinctive red tail**

McGee also accumulated his fair share of war stories, including one that occurred "during the bombing mission to the Czechoslovakian oil refinery at Pardubice, north of Vienna...Their tactic on that occasion was to try to fly through the bomber stream and keep on going. We were pretty much over the target area when we spotted a Focke Wulf Fw-190 and I got the word, 'Go get him.' I fell in behind him, and he took all kinds of evasive action, diving for the ground. We were down over the local airfield–I remember seeing a hangar on fire out of the corner of my eye–when I got in behind him and got in a burst that must have hit something in the controls. He took a couple more hard evasive turns and then went right into the ground. I stayed low getting out, to stay out of the sights of enemy groundfire. During that time, I saw a train pulling into a little station, so I dropped my nose and made a firing pass at the engine. Then, when I thought I'd pulled away from where I thought all the ack-ack was, I began climbing back up. Romine was my wingman on that occasion, and somewhere in all that jinking he had lost me and had gone up to rejoin the formation. He saw the Fw-190 crash, though, and confirmed the victory for me. [McGee's opponent was from Jagdgeschwader 300, three of whose Pardubice-based Fw-190As attacked the 5th Bomb Division and damaged two bombers before being driven off.] The 302nd's 1st Lt. William H. Thomas got another Fw-190 and 1st Lt. John F. Briggs of the 100th Squadron downed an Me-109 on that mission. Unfortunately, Romine got killed after his 97th mission–in an on-the-ground accident in his airplane–in November 1944."

Perhaps the Tuskegee Airmen's greatest accomplishment occurred on March 24, 1945, when Colonel Davis led 43 P-51s into battle to protect B-17 bombers destined for a round trip mission to Germany. The planes flew more than 1,600 miles that day to bomb the Daimler-Benz factory in Berlin, and during the mission, the Luftwaffe came after the bombers, hoping to defend the factory. Brown and others shot down a number of German fighters that day and saw to it that the bombers got through. For his part, Brown would go on to assert, "High-altitude escort was probably the most important plane in the war and shortened the war by about six months because it enabled the bombers to go a longer distance into Germany and destroy their infrastructure— their rail hubs, oil refineries, and so on. As a result, we didn't shoot down many planes, although on the longest mission of the 15th Air Force, from southern Italy to Berlin, we shot down the first jet planes in the 15th Air Force—the German Me-262—and I was the one who shot down the first of those jets. It was the first plane I'd shot down before. We used a maneuver that we'd been practicing, where when the jets were coming up, instead of going right after the jets so they could get away from us, cause they were faster, I went down under the bombers away from the jets, made a hard right turn so I could put the jet into my gun sight, and boom. It was a good maneuver because the jets were faster than we were, but we were more maneuverable."

That day, the 99th won its third Distinguished Unit Citation, this time for protecting their charges from an attack by German aircraft during one of the longest bomber escort missions of World War II. Needless to say, it was clear that George Marshall's decision to delay removing the 99th from active service proved wise. As noted by the "Air Force Officers Personnel Policy Development, 1944-1977," "Subsequent events validated Marshall's decision. In January 1944, the 99th ended its slump by destroying nine aircraft in a single day while supporting the invasion of Italy. Shortly thereafter, the all-black 332d Fighter Group, with Davis as its commander, entered the fray to provide fighter escort for bomber formations attacking targets in Europe. Flying better aircraft (P-51s) and with a cadre of experienced leaders, the 332d acquitted itself well, winning several unit combat decorations and never losing a bomber to enemy fighters. In the process, the unit destroyed over two hundred fifty enemy aircraft, more than six hundred pieces of rolling stock, and approximately forty ships and boats." The 99th even set an Air Corps record for shooting down five German planes in less than four minutes.

Of course, such a record came with a price, as being in the thick of aerial fighting ensured plenty of losses and close calls. Roscoe Brown vividly remembered his own: "I had some close calls. Once, when I was shooting a train on the ground, I hit the train and knocked off half my wing but was able to fly the plane back. Another time, I was shooting a locomotive and it blew up, and some of the stuff got in my air scoop, but I managed to fly it back. My plane also took a few bullets when I was doing ground support in Greece while liberating the Athens airport." McGee had similar stories: "[O]n some days, we were assigned a fighter sweep over an enemy airfield to go in and catch anything we could there. I was only credited with destroying one, but we damaged a great number of enemy aircraft on the ground. I flew a total of 136 [missions], of which 82 were tactical and 54 were long-range, high-altitude missions. I flew my last mission over Brux, Germany, on November 17, 1944, and it was a long one–about five hours, 45 minutes. Then, on November 23, I was shipped back to Tuskegee to replace a white twin-engine instructor. Training was now taking place for the 477th Bomb Group. I learned a number of years later that in 1945 the 302nd was disbanded; the 332nd went back to being a three-squadron group and its aircraft were assigned to the other squadrons. My Kitten went to the 301st Squadron, was renumbered 51 and flown by Lieutenant Leon Speers, who was shot down on April 24, 1945, and taken prisoner."

### Chapter 6: The Sad Story of the 477th

"The success of the 99th and 332d was in marked contrast to the sad story of the 477th Bombardment Group (M) (Colored). Activated in January 1944 as a medium (B-25) bomber unit, the 477th was doomed from the start. Always short of rated officers, particularly navigators and bombardiers, the number of crews never approached the quantity required. Over a year passed before the AAF made any effort whatsoever to do something about these shortages. Moved three times in fourteen months to find more suitable training conditions and to escape the hostility of local populations, the unit found its training constantly interrupted. The white staff proved so insensitive to racial matters that morale suffered badly. In April 1945, a number of black officers were arrested for trying to force their way into the only officers' club available, a club reserved for whites." – An excerpt from "Air Force Officers Personnel Policy Development, 1944-1977."

While many Tuskegee Airmen were fighting the Nazis in Europe, the 447th Bombardment

Group was waging a different kind of war at home. While training at Selfridge, an airbase outside of Detroit, the black pilots and officers chafed under the strict rules imposed by Colonel Robert Selway and Major General Frank Hunter. Hunter, commander of the First Air Force and thus responsible for all training in the United States, insisted on strict segregation of officer accommodations in all Air Corps facilities. In a short briefing given to the officers assigned to Selfridge, Hunter stated, "The War Department is not ready to recognize blacks on the level of social equal to white men. This is not the time for blacks to fight for equal rights or personal advantages. They should prove themselves in combat first. There will be no race problem here, for I will not tolerate any mixing of the races. Anyone who protests will be classed as an agitator, sought out, and dealt with accordingly. This is my base and, as long as I am in command, there will be no social mixing of the white and colored officers. The single Officers Club on base will be used solely by white officers. You colored officers will have to wait until an Officers Club is built for your use."

**Hunter**

Hunter's policy actually contradicted Army Regulation 210-10, Paragraph 19, which stated in part, "No officers club, mess, or other similar social organization of officers will be permitted by the post commander to occupy any part of any public building, other than the private quarters of an officer, unless such club, mess, or other organization extends to all officers on duty at the post the right to full membership, either permanent or temporary, in such club, mess, or organization, including the right equally with any and all other members thereof to participate in the management thereof, in which the officers concerned have an interest." While it did not do so explicitly, the regulation did have the effect of prohibiting racial segregation of officer facilities, so when the War Department learned that the Selfridge Officers Club was closed to black officers, the base commander, Colonel William Boyd, received an official reprimand.

The 477th's situation deteriorated on May 5, 1944 when the unit was suddenly relocated to Godman Field at Fort Knox, Kentucky. No explanation was given for the move, but it's altogether possible that Air Corps leadership feared a repeat of the summer 1943 race riot in Detroit and a deleterious effect on the morale and discipline on the all-black unit. The Officers Club at Godman was open to blacks, but most white officers used the club at Fort Knox as guest members, meaning they were technically the guest of one of the Army officers stationed at the Fort. This contributed to continuing poor morale among the men of the 477th, along with the unsuitability of the airfield for the B-25 and the lack of command advancement by black officers. By this time, the latter numbers included combat veterans of the 332nd Fighter Group who had transferred in, and naturally, the veterans who had earned the respect of white pilots through their proven combat skills in Europe did not take too well to having to fight for what they saw as their rightful due.

In spite of the difficulties, the 477th reached full combat strength by early 1945, being by that time composed of 616th, 617th, 618th, and 619th Bombardment Squadrons. Since it was scheduled to enter combat on July 1, it was relocated to Freeman Army Airfield in Indiana, a base with the facilities necessary for use by the B-25.

However, trouble began soon after the 477th moved to Freeman Field. The remaining African American officers at Godman learned that Colonel Selway had created two Officers Clubs at Freeman Field. Club Number One was for the use of trainees, while Club Number Two was to be used by instructors, but while technically not segregated by race, the fact that all trainees at the field were black and all instructors were white meant that the clubs were racially segregated.

**A picture of Selway facing Hubert L. Jones during a review of the 618th Bomber Squadron in Indiana**

A young Second Lieutenant and experienced union activist named Coleman Young (the future mayor of Detroit) brought together a group of black officers at Godman, and together, they decided to challenge the de facto segregation when they arrived at Freeman Field. The protests began on April 5; late in the afternoon, the final group of black officers from Godman arrived at Freeman, and they began to go to Club Number Two in small groups to seek service. The first group was turned away by the officer in charge of the club, and later groups were met by the Officer of the Day, who had been stationed there on orders of Colonel Selway.

Finally, 19 of the black officers led by Coleman Young entered the club and refused to leave, and in response, Major Andrew White, the officer in charge of Club Number Two, placed them under arrest "in quarters." The 19 of them left the club and returned to their quarters, but 17 additional officers were placed under arrest that night. One of them, Second Lieutenant Roger Terry, was accused by the Officer of the Day of shoving him.

**Terry**

The protests continued into the next night, with 25 more officers entering the club and being placed under arrest. Except for the one accusation of shoving, the protests were without violence, yet over the two-day protest, a total of 61 black officers were arrested.

**A picture of arrested black officers awaiting transport from Freeman Field back to Godman Field**

In response, the Air Force ordered an investigation, and in his report on the incident, Colonel Torgils C. Wold, the First Air Force's Air Inspector, determined that there was uncertainty about whether the order segregating the clubs had been properly drafted and published. Due to this uncertainty and the chance that the incident could have arisen from a misunderstanding, Wold recommended that charges be dropped against all officers except Lieutenant Terry and two others who were arrested with him. Colonel Selway, upon consultation with General Hunter, accepted the Air Inspector's recommendation and released 58 of the officers.

However, the issue did not end there. Taking the Air Inspector's findings concerning the original order to heart, Colonel Selway drafted Base Regulation 85-2. This regulation explicitly set forth the facilities which were to be used by trainees and those for the use of instructors. The regulation then stated, "Officers, Flight Officers and Warrant Officer personnel undergoing OTU, Combat Crew and Ground and Air Replacement Training will not enter buildings or use tennis courts listed in paragraph 3b, except on official business and with prior approval of the Base Commander, Deputy Base Commander, Director for Administration and Services, Director for Maintenance and Supply or Director of Operations and Training. After normal duty hours, such approval will be obtained through the Field Officer of the Day." To make sure there were no future "misunderstandings," the regulation also mandated that it must "be distributed to each officer presently assigned or assigned in the future to Freeman Field and will be read by each officer and returned to this Headquarters, certifying that he has read the order and that he fully understands it."

After issuing the order, Colonel Selway ordered his deputy commander, Lieutenant Colonel John B. Patterson, to assemble the trainees and read them the regulation. This was done on April 10, after which each officer was given a copy of the regulation and told to sign a statement certifying that they had read it and understood it. Each officer refused to sign. Squadron E's commander, Captain Anthony Chiappe, attempted to persuade 14 officers to sign, but only three did.

Faced with a situation bordering on insubordination, Colonel Selway consulted with his superiors, and upon their recommendations, he set up a board consisting of two black officers and two white officers. They were given the task of interviewing the non-signers individually. Each of the non-signers was given the option of signing the certification, signing their own individual certificates that did not have to acknowledge they understood the regulation, or face court martial under Article of War 64 for disobeying a direct order by a superior officer in time of war, an offence that could be punishable by death. The board interviewed the officers on April 11, and 101 refused to sign and were placed under arrest and returned to Godman Field for trial. African American organizations, labor unions, and members of Congress pressured the War Department to drop the charges, and on April 23, Chief of Staff General George C. Marshall ordered their release, but even after the charges were dropped, General Hunter placed an administrative reprimand in the files of each of the officers.

The final legal issues arising from the original protests were resolved in July when Lieutenant Terry and Second Lieutenants Marsden Thompson and Shirley Clinton received a general court-martial for shoving Lieutenant Rogers on the night of April 5. Their defense team included future associate Supreme Court justice Thurgood Marshall and the future mayor of Cincinnati, Theodore M. Berry. Thompson and Clinton were acquitted, but Terry was convicted of shoving Lieutenant Rogers; he was fined $150 dollars, suffered loss of rank, and received a dishonorable discharge.

**Marshall**

After the protests, the 477th was relocated to Godman Field. The 616th and the 619th were deactivated, and now that the war in Europe was over, the 99th was added to the group, which was designated as the 477th Composite Group on June 22, 1945. Colonel Benjamin O. Davis, Jr., took command of the group on July 1. Training was to be completed by August 31, but the war ended on August 14 when Japan surrendered. In 1946, the 477th was reassigned to Lockbourne Field in Ohio, but it was made inactive in 1947.

### Chapter 7: Unique Military Record

"An Act to award a congressional gold medal on behalf of the Tuskegee Airmen, collectively, in recognition of their unique military record, which inspired revolutionary reform in the Armed Forces. Be it enacted by the Senate and House of Representatives of the United States of America in Congress Assembled…The Congress finds the following (1) In 1941, President Franklin D. Roosevelt overruled his top generals and ordered the creation of an all Black flight training program. President Roosevelt took this action one day after the NAACP filed suit on behalf of Howard University student Yancy Williams and others in Federal court to force the Department of War to accept Black pilot trainees. (2) Due to the rigid system of racial segregation that prevailed in the United States during World War II, Black military pilots were trained at a separate airfield built near Tuskegee, Alabama. They became known as the ``Tuskegee Airmen''.... The Speaker of the House of Representatives and the President pro tempore of the Senate shall make appropriate arrangements for the award, on behalf of the Congress, of a single gold medal of appropriate design in honor of the Tuskegee Airmen, collectively, in recognition of their unique military record, which inspired revolutionary reform in the Armed Forces." - Text from the Joint Congressional Resolution to give the Tuskegee Airmen the Congressional Gold Medal

In spite of the sad story of the 477th, the Tuskegee Airmen greatly contributed to the Air Corps' efforts in Europe and undoubtedly proved themselves to be the equal of white airmen. 992 pilots were trained in Tuskegee between 1941 and 1946, and of these, 355 saw combat over the skies of Southern Europe. In all, 68 pilots were killed in action, 12 were killed in training or non-combat missions, and 32 were captured as prisoners of war. The Airmen were credited with the following accomplishments:

- 1578 combat missions, 1267 for the Twelfth Air Force; 311 for the Fifteenth Air Force
- 179 bomber escort missions, losing bombers on only seven missions and a total of only 27
- 262 enemy aircraft destroyed (112 in the air,150 on the ground) and 148 damaged
- 950 rail cars, trucks and other motor vehicles destroyed
- One destroyer put out of action.
- 40 boats and barges destroyed

The Tuskegee Airmen received recognition at the time for their service. Collectively, the Airmen received three Distinguished Unit Citations. Two were for actions over Sicily and Italy, and the third one, given to the 332d Fighter Group, was awarded for a bomber escort mission to Berlin on March 24, 1945, during which pilots shot down three Me-262 fighters, the world's first operational jet fighters. Individual pilots distinguished themselves as well; pilots were awarded one Silver Star, 95 Distinguished Flying Cross medals, 14 Bronze Stars, 744 Air Medals, and 8 Purple Hearts.

The Tuskegee Airmen's record regarding bomber escorts has been the subject of controversy for almost 70 years. It began with a March 24, 1945 article published in the *Chicago Defender* headlined "332d Flies its 200th Mission without Loss," which claimed that no bomber ever escorted by the Tuskegee Airmen had been lost to enemy fire. This statement was repeated over the years primarily because the mission reports remained classified, but by the early 21st century, the mission reports were declassified and research began into the Tuskegee Airmen's record. In 2006, Dr. Daniel Haulman of the Air Force Historical Research Agency conducted a reassessment of the history of the unit. His report, based on the after-mission reports, missing air crew records, and witness testimony, documented 25 bombers shot down by enemy fighter aircraft. His research was further presented in an article, "The Tuskegee Airmen and the Never Lost a Bomber Myth," published in *The Alabama Review*, as well as a comprehensive study that documented 27 bombers shot down while being escorted by the 332d Fighter Group, including 15 B-17s lost in a savage duel with 300 German fighters on July 18, 1944. That said, when compared with other P-51 fighter groups in the 15th Air Force, it's clear that the Tuskegee Airmen's record needed no exaggeration, as their 27 lost was far below the average of 46.

The myth of the Tuskegee Airmen's "never lost a bomber record" was only one myth, or rather misconception, that grew up around the Airmen either at the time or later. Haulman, in a paper titled "Misconceptions about the Tuskegee Airmen," has documented 40 various myths, including the following:

- The misconception of the deprived ace
- The misconception of being first to shoot down German jets
- The misconception that the Tuskegee Airmen sank a German destroyer
- The misconception that the Tuskegee Airmen units were all black
- The misconception that all Tuskegee Airmen were fighter pilots who flew red-tailed P-51s to escort bombers
- The misconception that after a flight with a black pilot at Tuskegee, Eleanor Roosevelt persuaded the President to establish a black flying unit in the Army Air Corps
- The misconception that the Tuskegee Airmen were the first to implement a "stick with the bombers" policy
- The misconception that the 332nd Fighter Group was the only one to escort Fifteenth Air Force bombers over Berlin
- The misconception that the training of black pilots for combat was an experiment designed to fail.
- The misconception that the outstanding World War II record of the Tuskegee Airmen alone convinced President Truman to desegregate the armed forces of the United States
- The misconception that the Tuskegee Airmen were the only fighter pilots following the official policy of "sticking with the bombers"
- The misconception that the Tuskegee Airmen's 332nd Fighter Group flew more different kinds of aircraft in combat than any other Army Air Forces group during World War II
- The misconception that the Tuskegee Airmen belonged to some of the most highly decorated units in U.S. military history
- The misconception that the Tuskegee Airmen never got the recognition they deserved

- The misconception that Tuskegee Airman Charles McGee flew more combat missions than any other pilot in the Air Force
- The misconception that Daniel "Chappie" James, the first four-star black general in the U.S. military services, was among the leaders of the "Freeman Field Mutiny" in April 1945
- The misconception that the Tuskegee Airmen's 332nd Fighter Group flew more combat missions than any other unit in Europe during World War II
- The misconception that Col. Benjamin O. Davis, Jr., by ordering his pilots to "stick with the bombers," put his pilots in greater danger than the white pilots, and gave them less opportunity to become aces
- The misconception that black organizations and black newspapers all supported the training of black pilots at Tuskegee
- The misconception that the Tuskegee Airmen won the 1949 USAF gunnery meet in Las Vegas, defeating all other fighter groups in the Air Force
- The misconception that Tuskegee Airman Daniel "Chappie" James was an ace
- The misconception that Tuskegee Airman Benjamin O. Davis, Jr. graduated top in his class at the United States Military Academy at West Point
- The misconception that each of the Tuskegee Airmen was awarded a Congressional Gold Medal, or that they were each awarded the Medal of Honor
- The misconception that when the Tuskegee Airmen returned to the United States after combat overseas, no one welcomed them
- The misconception that the Tuskegee Airmen were instrumental in the defeat of German forces in North Africa.

Why did these misconceptions arise? The best explanation may have come from the man who was so instrumental in training the Tuskegee Airmen. In a 1947 thesis he wrote for the Air Command and Staff School, Colonel Noel F. Parrish, the commander of the basic and advanced flying school at Tuskegee Army Air Field, pointed to segregation itself as a factor: "Each establishment of a 'Negro Unit' project was finally covered with a smoke screen of praise which clouded the issues and obscured the facts…[Black units] gathered more than necessary praise…military men showed an overwhelming tendency to believe, repeat and exaggerate all the stories…Such a situation [segregation] leads to an exaggeration of both the honors and the defamations."

Exaggerated claims or not, the Tuskegee Airmen carried out the missions they were given during World War II, but the mission of the Tuskegee Airmen did not end with the war either. Their combat record quieted many of those who claimed that African Americans would not make good pilots, and along with the performances of minorities in other military branches during World War II, they helped pave the way for President Harry S. Truman's integration of the military in 1948 with Executive Order 9981. Roscoe Brown summed up what many of the Tuskegee Airmen no doubt thought: "This country was built on race, racial prejudice, and the efforts of blacks. So blacks have fought in every war going back to the Revolutionary War. Each time that we did that, we thought that if we defended the country and did it with dignity and excellence, the broader community would end segregation. After World War II, that finally happened when in 1948, President Truman signed Executive Order 9981 eliminating segregation in the armed forces. So in a sense we made that progress."

Once the military was integrated, the veterans then found themselves in high demand in the newly-formed independent United States Air Force as they were reassigned to formerly all-white units. Some who had left the military taught future pilots in civilian flight schools, and one of the Tuskegee Airmen, Daniel "Chappie" James, Jr., who had been an instructor and fighter pilot with the 99th, became the first African American to achieve the rank of four-star general in 1975.

**James**

With the passage of time, many of the achievements of the Tuskegee Airmen have faded into the past, and many veterans of the unit have been forgotten. In this way, they were no different than other veterans of World War II whose service in the most destructive war in the history of mankind went underappreciated for several decades after 1945. Particularly during the 1960s and 1970s, with unrest caused by protests against the Vietnam War, little interest was shown in what American men and women of all races had done during another war.

However, with the revival of patriotism in the 1980s and the 50th anniversary commemorations during the 1990s, Americans turned to the members of the Greatest Generation to show their appreciation and their gratitude. The Tuskegee Airmen were particular beneficiaries of this renewed interest in the sacrifices of the soldiers, sailors and airmen who fought tyranny and fascism in the 1940s, and aside from their military exploits, their pivotal role in changing attitudes about race relations and laying the groundwork for the Civil Rights Movement also drew focus. There was a sense that, as black men serving in a segregated military during the Jim Crow era of American history, they deserved more than their share of recognition and honors. In 1998, Moton Field was named a National Historical Site and placed on the National Register of Historic Places. In 2006, the United States Postal Service issued a commemorative postage stamp, and on August 1, 2008, the state of Georgia renamed a portion of State Route 6 in south Fulton County and in the City of East Point in honor of the Airmen.

Of all the honors the remaining members of the Tuskegee Airmen have received, certainly the greatest was the Congressional Gold Medal awarded on March 29, 2007 in a ceremony in the Capitol rotunda. The Congressional Resolution authorizing the medal stated, "The Tuskegee Airmen inspired revolutionary reform in the Armed Forces, paving the way for full racial integration in the Armed Forces. They overcame the enormous challenges of prejudice and discrimination, succeeding, despite obstacles that threatened failure." The Congressional Gold Medal is now on display at the Smithsonian Institution's National Air and Space Museum.

In his remarks on the occasion, President George W. Bush summed up the Tuskegee Airmen's contributions, both to the war effort and the cause of racial equality:

> "I have a strong interest in World War II airmen; I was raised by one. He flew with a group of brave young men who endured difficult times in the defense of our country.

> "Yet for all they sacrificed and all they lost, in a way, they were very fortunate, because they never had the burden of having their every mission, their every success, their every failure viewed through the color of their skin. Nobody told them they were a credit to their race. Nobody refused to return their salutes. Nobody expected them to bear the daily humiliations while wearing the uniform of their country.

> "It was different for the men in this room. When America entered World War II, it might have been easy for them to do little for our country. After all, the country didn't do much for them. Even the Nazis asked why African American men would fight for a country that treated them so unfairly. Yet the Tuskegee Airmen were eager to join up.

> "You know, I'm interested in the story about a young man who was so worried that the Army might change its mind about allowing him to fly, that he drove immediately to the train station. He left his car, as well as $1,000 worth of

photography equipment. He never saw his car, he never saw his camera, but he became a flyer.

"These men in our presence felt a special sense of urgency. They were fighting two wars: One was in Europe, and the other took place in the hearts and minds of our citizens. That's why we're here. ...

"Soon, Americans in their kitchens and living rooms were reading the headlines. You probably didn't realize it at the time, but you were making headlines at home, headlines that spoke about daring pilots winning a common battle.

"And little by little, every victory at war was translated to a victory here in the United States. And we're in the presence of men who are earning those victories, important victories, leaders who pierced the unquestioned prejudices of a different society. You gave African Americans a sense of pride and possibility.

"You saw that pride and awe—I'm sure you remember—in the faces of young children who came up to you right after the war and tugged on your uniforms and said, ''Mister, can you really fly an airplane?'' ...

"...I appreciate the fact that one of our soldiers today said: ''It is not often that you get a chance to meet the guys who have paved the path for you.''

"The Tuskegee Airmen helped win a war, and you helped change our Nation for the better. Yours is the story of the human spirit, and it ends like all great stories do— with wisdom and lessons and hope for tomorrow. And the medal that we confer today means that we're doing a small part to ensure that your story will be told and honored for generations to come.

"And I would like to offer a gesture to help atone for all the unreturned salutes and unforgivable indignities. And so, on behalf of the Office I hold and a country that honors you, I salute you for the service to the United States of America."

While there is no way to know for sure, the Tuskegee Airmen, Incorporated, the organization for veterans of the African American flying units, estimates that there are only around 200 former squadron members still alive. But even as their numbers dwindle, their legacy continues to resonate in the experiences of the men and women of all races who serve in the military.

**Online Resources**

Other books about World War II by Charles River Editors

Other books about the Tuskegee Airmen on Amazon

**Bibliography**

Broadnax, Samuel L. Blue Skies, Black Wings: African American Pioneers of Aviation. Westport, Connecticut: Praeger Publishers, 2007.

Bucholtz, Chris and Jim Laurier. 332nd Fighter Group – Tuskegee Airmen. Oxford, UK: Osprey Publishing, 2007.

Francis, Charles E. and Adolph Caso. The Tuskegee Airmen: The Men Who Changed a Nation. Boston: Branden Books, 1997.

Holway, John B. Red Tail, Black Wings: The Men of America's Black Air Force. Las Cruces, New Mexico: Yuca Tree Press, 1997.

Haulman, Daniel L. Eleven Myths About the Tuskegee Airmen. Montgomery, Alabama: New South Books, 2012.

Homan, Lynn M. and Thomas Reilly. Black Knights: The Story of the Tuskegee Airmen. Gretna, Louisiana: Pelican Publishing, 2001.

Moye, J. Todd. Freedom Flyers: The Tuskegee Airmen of World War II. New York: Oxford University Press (USA), 2010.

Ross, Robert A. Lonely Eagles: The Story of America's Black Air Force in World War II. Los Angeles: Tuskegee Airmen Inc., Los Angeles Chapter, 1980.

Sandler, Stanley. Segregated Skies: All-Black Combat Squadrons of WWII. Washington, D.C.: Smithsonian Institution Press, 1992.